Living in Consciousness Workbook

Use What U Know About U

Paula Heller-Garland
University of North Texas

Kendall Hunt
publishing company

Cover image courtesy of Jack D. Schrader

Kendall Hunt
publishing company

www.kendallhunt.com
Send all inquiries to:
4050 Westmark Drive
Dubuque, IA 52004-1840

ISBN 978-1-4652-1977-0

Printed in the United States of America
10 9 8 7 6 5 4 3 2

Table of Contents

Thanks

From Paula: I have grown a great deal in the process of working on this book. I am grateful to Tyrone Carrington for his dedication to diving deep into the process without knowing where the journey would lead and his challenging me to become a better human being.

Heartfelt thanks to my Sonshine for the support and encouragement shown daily to this mother, who he believes is better than I could ever deserve. I love you to the moon.

Thanks to countless staff and students at The University of North Texas who have devoted time, energy and feedback to the development of Living in Consciousness.

From Tyrone: I want to first thank Paula Heller Garland for unlocking the story of me and giving me an arena to explore who I really am. I have wanted to be a better person and understand my history for a long while but had not gotten there yet. Paula, you gave me the nudge I needed and I will keep it with me to the grave. I have learned the power of sharing when I reach a person and know that I have given back so someone can be better with what they know about themselves. Use what U know about U!

I can't put into words what my mother, Eartha Carrington, means to me. The vision and patience she has shown over the years is incredible. For her to believe early on that I was capable of what I am doing today is what I call a vision. My strength and my drive are what I give for what she has done for me. Thank you, Mommz, the soul survivor. She still loves and cares!

Foreword

con·scious **kon**-sh*uhs] adjective*

1. aware of one's own existence, sensations, thoughts, surroundings, etc.
2. fully aware of or sensitive to something (often followed by of): conscious of one's own faults; He wasn't conscious of the gossip about his past.
3. having the mental faculties fully active: He was conscious during the operation.
4. known to oneself; felt: conscious guilt.
5. aware of what one is doing: a conscious liar.

Is this for you?

If you already have everything you want in life, this work is not for you. If you are 100% satisfied with the outcome in your daily life and have no areas you wish to improve, this work is not for you. For everyone else…this work will explore the person you are and encourage you in setting and meeting the goals necessary for you to become who you wish to be. It will journey you through the foundation of how you have become the person you are today and allow you to easily see how your experiences greatly shape that person. Furthermore, you will see how adamantly your experiences, beliefs and ideas speak for you to others in your life, often leaving you to wonder how you ended up in the same situation again…even if not with the same people.

Intention:

Getting to the place you want in life involves interactions with others. Our experiences drive most of our behavior. Beliefs are important. But have you taken a look at how they impact your functioning with others? If you'd like to be in a better place – happier or more successful, for example, or working more effectively toward meeting your goals – it might benefit you to take a look at who you are, how you became that person, who you want to be and what it will take to get there. That requires living life consciously.

The big challenge is to remain flexible for what life has to offer, even if it is not always good; be flexible enough to not bend, not break.

The only requirement: to remain open.

Meet Tyrone

Throughout the workbook, there will be excerpts of interviews with Tyrone Carrington.

Tyrone volunteered to answer the questions in the workbook and be interviewed. He didn't realize when he began this journey what he would discover. Tyrone took the book very seriously and ultimately; it led him on a path of personal change and growth he never imagined.

Interview*One*

Paula: Welcome, Tyrone. How are you?

Tyrone: I am doing well.

Paula: Let's get started with the book! If someone asked you to describe yourself, would you say you are?

Tyrone: I'm a hippie. I have passion and vision. I am loyal. In a business setting I would describe myself as being a confident, efficient worker. I always want to learn more. I work with a passion. I am personable, I communicate well. I'm a talker. But I suck at selling.

In a social setting I am an inviting person. People seem to feel comfortable to engage me. I seem to be able to communicate and believe I foster an opportunity to let people talk. I am usually holding my hand out to say hello. I am not into being "scene king" like I was when I was younger, but to being more into networking now.

To a potential romantic partner I hope someone would take away that I am attractive, sound and have my shit together and I think I am confident but not cocky.

Throughout all of the settings the characteristic that is solid throughout my life is having a positive attitude. I am also loyal in all areas. The characteristic that is weak in one area but not in another is networking. There seems to be an underlying tone of my lack of desire not to network if I don't believe in something. But in my personal life I can network and socialize well with people.

When I describe myself I use characteristics more than roles.

Paula: Tell me about the most important things in your life.

Tyrone: People, places or things?

Paula: Any.

Tyrone: My mommz, trips I took to Canada, Portland and Pueblo. The day my mommz came to Texas. The car crash I had when I was 25. My friends Robin, Jerrit, Phillip and Paula.

I learned something from everyone I mentioned, and the trips were important but the people are most valuable.

To discover the person you are, attempt to be spontaneous with your responses. Write down the first thoughts that come to mind instead of overthinking.

Who are you?

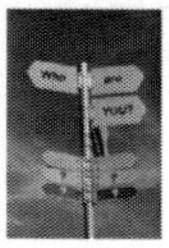

If you were introducing yourself to someone new, how would you describe yourself?

How would you describe yourself in the following different settings:

Business Settings:

Social Settings:

To a potential romantic interest:

Talk about how the characteristics you use to describe yourself are similar and different?

Did you use roles or characteristics to describe yourself? Explain.

List the 10 most important involvements in your life. Include people, places, things, events; anything that you consider a priority.

After you list the top ten priorities, mark out the least important five.

Then, list the top five in the order of importance.

Next, beside each, indicate how long it has been since you have engaged with each.

Finally, indicate how much money each costs when you engage.

How did it feel to pick the most important five?

What caused you to pick the top five?

What evidence exists that these are priorities?

When you value something or someone, you spend time engaging with them. When they are healthy engagements they bring joy to your life and don't require a great deal of financial investment.

Talk about how your priorities bring you joy.

Discuss the priorities you don't spend time pursuing or nurturing.

Talk about an occasion when you used the excuse that you couldn't do something because it was too expensive, but it actually was not.

Do you believe you are more selfish or selfless? Explain.

How does this help you?

How does it hurt you?

Speak to how you balance selfishness and selflessness to get your needs met and some of your wants accomplished in ways that are not harmful to others.

Behaviors:

Beliefs about yourself or others:

To explore your beliefs, write down the very first thought you have. Do not attempt to write the "right" answer. There is no right or wrong in this workbook.

What do you believe?

Beside each photo, jot down thoughts or feelings that come to mind when you see it.

By sharing with others, notice how people respond differently to these images. What does that mean to you?

Talk about the beliefs you hold most strongly.

Why are these beliefs so important to you?

Complete the following statements:

I can't stand ________

I hate it when ________

I love it when ________

I will never ________

I will always ________

The world feels right when ________

Do you think your beliefs are right? Explain.

Do you believe others who do not agree with you are wrong? Explain.

How do your beliefs come into conflict with others in your life?

If you are speeding down the highway and get pulled over, do you believe you are wrong or right? Explain the reason for your answer.

What makes a behavior or belief right or wrong, in your opinion?

What are the beliefs that guide your life?

Evidence of your beliefs shows up in how you live your life daily.

What is your evidence that you believe those things?

What is your evidence?

When we believe something we generally live our lives accordingly. How can we prove we believe something, if not by living that belief? If we have beliefs we say we hold but do not live, is it possible those beliefs are no longer helpful?

How do your beliefs help you?

Sometimes when we believe something so strongly we say we hate it or we can't stand it, and by doing this, we limit ourselves. Limiting ourselves can be harmful. Interestingly, this often happens so quickly and unconsciously we do it without realizing we have.

How do your beliefs hurt you?

How do I behave as if these beliefs aren't important?

What is the payoff to holding onto your beliefs?

What is the consequence to holding onto your beliefs?

Interview*Two*

Paula: Tell me about what you've discovered you are through this workbook.

Tyrone: I learned a lot about my past through this activity. At first I answered the easy questions in this book. Then I decided to give myself a better opportunity so I answered all of them, really answered them.

Paula: Really answered them?

Tyrone: You know, instead of just saying what my favorite color is or skipping the hard questions, I answered them all honestly

Paula: What did you discover?

Tyrone: I wasn't set up to make good decisions. I was written to screw up.

Paula: Tell me about that.

Tyrone: Like most boys, I idolized my dad. I didn't know anything he was teaching me wouldn't be effective. But as I grew up he was really disabling me.

Paula: How?

Tyrone: He was a drill sergeant. He was trained in war and he was good at his job. He told groups of people what to do, how to do it and when to do it so they would survive. That made a great drill sergeant, but it didn't make a good father to a young boy. I never had to or even got to think for myself. I did what he told me to do. I didn't make any mistakes because I didn't get to choose for myself.

Paula: It sounds like you uncovered a lot of answers.

Tyrone: I answered the questions. One question I asked was, "How did I become me?"

Paula: That is a good question. How did you answer?

Tyrone: My Mommz, I call her "mommz" with a *z*, was the diffuser between my dad and me. So I wondered if it was the caring hand of my mother or the firm voice of dad, the enforcer, who made me who I was. I had to dig deep to find the answers. The goal is to have a balance of both. In my case the soothing voice of reason was Mommz. So I did the math.

Paula: What did you discover?

Tyrone: There was a lot of one-way communication. What dad said was law, very much like a dictator. There was no back and forth, as you would assume is normal in growing-up situations, and my influence or voice had no value.

Paula: How did that impact your relationships with others?

Tyrone: Growing up with this form of communication caused me to behave that way. Learning to share views and points of interest was difficult until I learned I cannot make my views law or right for every one around me, then it hit! It's okay for others to think differently and not think like me, and that's okay to accept I'm not always right. That was hard when I was raised with the "I am right all the time" laws in the house, that is, and that mind-set won't last long in the real world!

Paula: I bet that was difficult.

Tyrone: I was raised in Oklahoma on the farm. It was a great place to be raised. It was safe. It was the transition to the city masses, to people who were completely different than me that was hard. Finding it's okay for others to be different or even for me to like something I never had a thought about before. The core of who I am may come from that very place, the country, but the city and adversity molded my soul. Meaning going through all these things shaped what types of choices I would make, good and bad.

To live consciously it is important to know how you experience yourself.

How do you perceive yourself?

perception

How would you describe your strengths and weaknesses?

What do you like about yourself?

What do you dislike about yourself?

What would you change about yourself immediately if you had a magic wand?

What is your contribution to the world

What do you take from the world?

While you cannot live with the goal of making others happy, it is important to know your impact on the world around you.

How do others perceive you?

Discuss how two or three people who love you would describe you.

Person:

How would that person describe you?

Person:

How would that person describe you?

Person:

How would that person describe you?

What would others say they like about you?

What would people immediately change about you, if given the chance?

What would they say you contribute to the world?

What would they say you take from the world?

An important element to* Living in Consciousness *is realizing the differences between the person you think you are and how others actually experience you.

Incongruences between how you and others perceive you

What is the legacy you would leave today?

If your life were over today, what would be left to remember you

What is the legacy you want to leave

What would you have left undone

If you ever want to change the person you are, it is important to know the how and why related to how you became the person you are today.

How did you become who you are?

Describe the place you now refer to as home.

Describe the home in which you grew up.

Who raised you?

Where were you raised? City, state, country

What was it like?

In what era were you raised?

How does generation play a role

The person you are today was greatly influenced by your past experiences. Take a few minutes to discover the impact of your past.

What are your foundational elements and their impact?

Things you learn in your formative years usually become the foundation of your view of life. Before you bring these into your consciousness, it is possible some of these beliefs led to many of your decisions.

List the people who were part of your formative years and who you believe were an influence on your life.

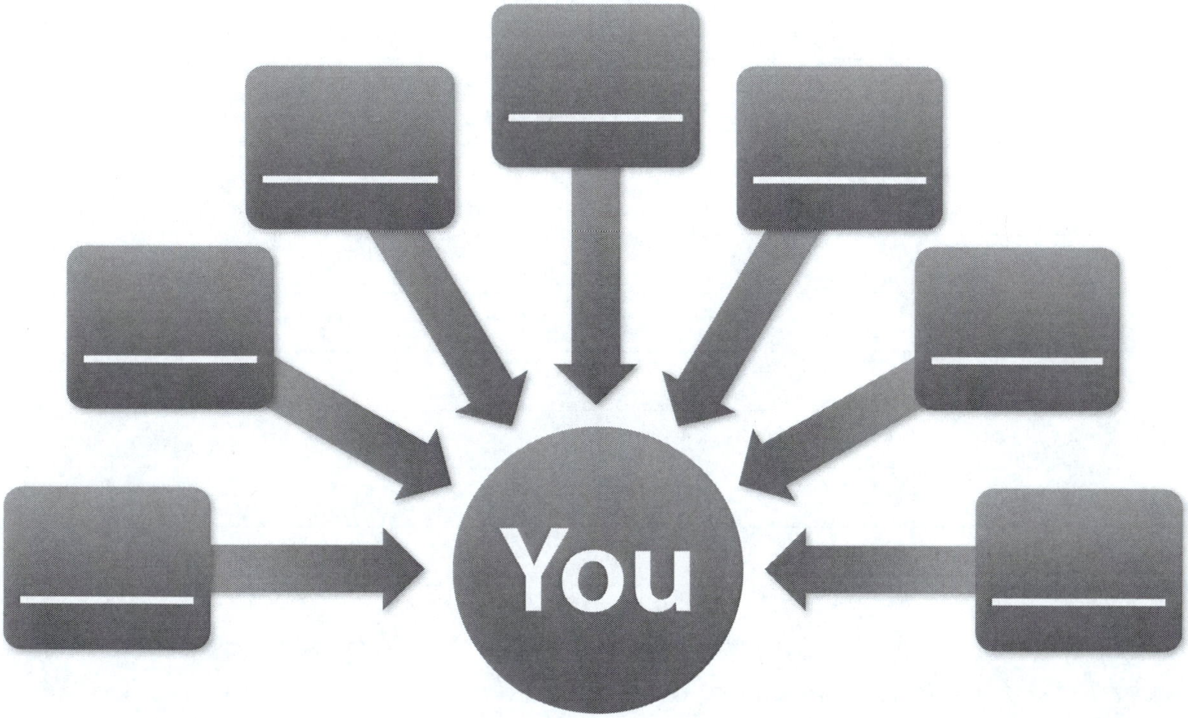

Talk about the people who influenced your formative years. Discuss who they were, if the influence was positive or negative, and any other thoughts and memories you have.

What events had an impact on your formative years?

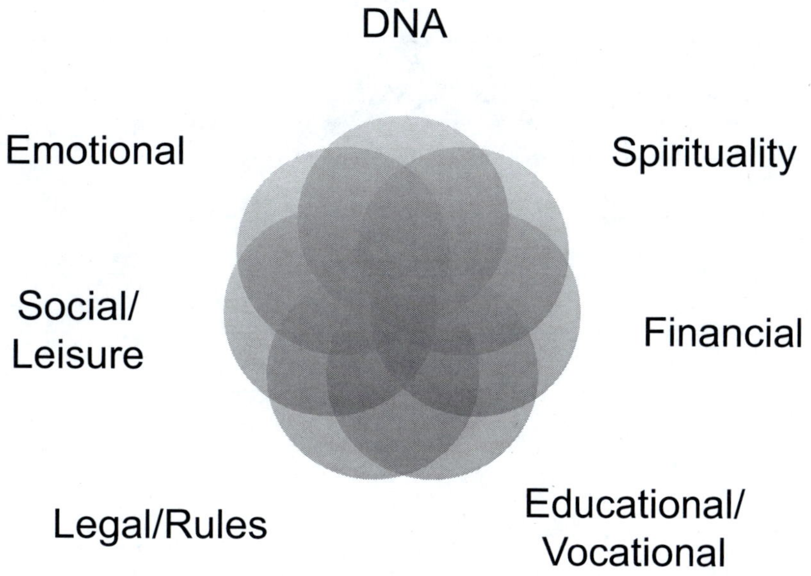

Take a look at your past. In the following areas, what did you learn?

DNA by heredity and practice

Some things, such as your height, eye color and family history of cancer, cannot be changed. What is in your family history?

The following are ***DNA inherited by experience***. They are historical facts of how you were raised. They influenced you a great deal. This is where beliefs come from. The history cannot be changed. But with work, the impact can be minimized. This is where you can change the future by Living in Consciousness of these categories.

Spirituality

What was the driving force of your family? A religion? A belief? A purpose? What were the positive and negative impacts on you

Financial

This is not about how much money your family had, but about the value that was placed on the money and how it was handled. Did your family struggle? Were items given in place of affection?

Educational

How was education viewed in your family? What were the expectations of you?

Vocational

What was the work ethic in your family? Was employment a high priority? Were you encouraged to pursue a particular vocation?

Legal/Rules

How were rules given and followed through with in your family? Were consequences punitive or too lenient? Was your family involved in the criminal justice system? What was their opinion of law enforcement?

Social/Leisure

What kinds of friendships did you form growing up? What types of activity did you participate in? What were their influences?

Emotional

How were feelings communicated in your family? Were you free to express them? Were there any feelings more predominant than others?

Example: Oftentimes in families who do not have experience in expressing emotion, children are stifled from understanding and expressing their emotions.

If a little boy's dog is run over, it is normal for that little boy to feel ________. If the little boy feels ________ he is likely to express it by ____________________________.

If an adult family member is uncomfortable with this feeling or expression of feeling they may shame the little boy for crying by saying something like, "Boys don't cry. Suck it up." So the little boy may confuse emotions and their expression in the future.

Talk about the feelings you were encouraged to express.

Talk about the feelings you were encouraged to suppress.

Discuss how this might interfere with your relationships today.

Take a look at the garden from which you sprang!

The fruit from the trees

Identify traits from your family.

Person: ______________________

Relationship to you: ______________________

Medical concerns:

Behavioral health concerns:

Personality traits:

Notable major life events:

___

___

___

Impact on your life:

___

___

___

Person: ___

Relationship to you: ___

Medical concerns:

___

___

___

Behavioral health concerns:

___

___

___

Personality traits:

___

___

___

Notable major life events:

___

___

___

Impact on your life:

Person: ______________________________

Relationship to you: ______________________________

Medical concerns:

Behavioral health concerns:

Personality traits:

Notable major life events:

Impact on your life:

Person: ______________________________

Relationship to you: ______________________________

Medical concerns:

____

____

____

Behavioral health concerns:

____

____

____

Personality traits:

____

____

____

Notable major life events:

____

____

____

Impact on your life:

____

____

____

Person: ______________________________

Relationship to you: ______________________________

Medical concerns:

____

Behavioral health concerns:

Personality traits:

Notable major life events:

Impact on your life:

Person:

Relationship to you:

Medical concerns:

Behavioral health concerns:

Personality traits:

Notable major life events:

Impact on your life:

Person:

Relationship to you:

Medical concerns:

Behavioral health concerns:

Personality traits:

Notable major life events:

Impact on your life:

Person: ____________________

Relationship to you: ____________________

Medical concerns:

Behavioral health concerns:

Personality traits:

Notable major life events:

Impact on your life:

Interview Three

Paula: Tell me about the impact your childhood experiences had on your relationships.

Tyrone: I had to learn that I wasn't always right and that it was okay not to shut down. I know why I did, though, and that helps.

Paula: How does that help?

Tyrone: "Who am I" was a question I answered by looking at the how and the why of who I was. Living in Consciousness is using what I know about me to live better. If I discovered all those things about my history and never used any of that information it means nothing. Today I can apply that information and share it with others. I was only surviving for a lot of years. I can live now.

Paula: And how does that improve your relationships?

Tyrone: I am more patient. I can learn from others. I can share. I have an incredible relationship with my mommz. She knew we would get here one day. She believed in me before I believed in myself. Growing and sharing is a legacy I can leave of my life. When my mom was translating or defusing what my dad said to me, she was gentle. She helped me understand on some level. I know that saved me in the long run.

Our past experiences have a great deal of impact on our current relationships. If you find yourself generalizing groups of people as all bad it will pay off to take a look at your experiences first.

Relationships

What were your relationships like with those in your family?

Person: ______________________________

Describe your relationship.

____

____

____

____

____

____

____

Person: ____________________

Describe your relationship.

Person: ____________________

Describe your relationship.

Person: ____________________

Describe your relationship.

Whom could you trust? Whom were you unable to trust? What made relationships positive? Negative?

Oftentimes, due to past experiences, people generalize entire groups of people. For example, if you were hurt in a relationship in the past you may believe all (men, women, white people, poor people) are bad. When you interact with someone from that group now you may already limit your experience.

What beliefs do you currently hang onto

How important to you is it to hang onto those beliefs?

The best news about **Living in Consciousness** ***is you have control over who you become.***

What do you want to become?

The magic wand! You can't make someone love you who doesn't and you can't bring someone back to life who has passed away. Otherwise, if your biggest problem were solved, what would it be and what would your life look like?

What would your life look like if it could look exactly the way you want?

It's time to get out the map.

How do I get there from here?

What are the incongruences between who you are and who you want to be?

What is holding you back from getting what you want in life? What are the obstacles?

Circle those that are real, not imagined.

Mark through those that are excuses.

Circle the obstacles you could overcome, with some work.

If you were to change the foundation elements of your life, the inherited DNA, what would you change?

What can be overcome? What can you change? What can you not change? Who and what are the people and events over which you have no control?

What are you hanging onto that is beyond your control?

How is it paying off to hang on? You may immediately say it is not paying off. That isn't possible. You don't hang onto things that don't have a payoff. For example, if you had a bad relationship with your mother you may blame her for the person you are today. Hanging onto that blame keeps you from having to change and allows her to remain responsible for the person you are.

You cannot get from one point to the next without a plan.

Interview *Four*

Paula: Talk about the goal-setting work you did.

Tyrone: Now I realize it is all about sacrifice. If I want to accomplish a goal I have to ask myself, "How much will I sacrifice to get there?" So goal-setting is about setting the right goals, and the most important part is the work that it takes to get there. I can plan all day, but if I don't put in the work nothing is going to happen

Paula: Great point.

Tyrone: Goal-setting is about where I come from and the dreams I have had and if I am willing to do something about them. It depends on how focused I stay to that goal and what I will sacrifice to be great at something. Setting the right goals and playing to my strengths is important. I can never stop learning from my experiences.

Paula: What direction are you working now?

Tyrone: My mind is on making it, and I can make it with the tools I have that God has given me. My first priority is to get smarter than I was. My second priority is to focus on what I believe it will take to accomplish that, then practice and hard work — even losing a little sleep along the way, but having big payoffs in the future!

Paula: What else have you learned?

Tyrone: Goal-setting was a journey to understanding first what a long-term goal really is. By that I mean short-term goals filled my life in the past. I was not thinking about a month from now or a year from now. It never entered my brain to worry about anything farther than in front of me. I mean…no planning at all, just dealing with needs as they came: food, shelter and transportation. That is what I needed. This is just a small sample of my thought pattern. It did change when I willed or wanted it to change. I wanted more from me. What I am expressing now, is that at some point I wanted what others had so I had to create a plan on how to get it. For myself getting my hustle on is where I am growing more each day. I am reading books, getting into social groups and talking about the future. I am trying to put in work for the money! It's all about sacrifice.

Paula: Planning for the future but working today?

Tyrone: I ask myself, "How much will I sacrifice to get there?" So goal-setting is about setting the *right* goals. The most important part is the work that it takes to get there. I can plan all day but if I do not work, nothing is going to happen.

Paula: *Nodding.*

Tyrone: I also believe that in your early to late 20s the decision-making is critical to the rest of your life. How will it be lived and played out? Do you, as an individual, understand the choice that work now pays off later? Because I wasn't making those critical decisions in my 20s; it was more about party today and you will see what happens later!

Paula: How did that work out?

Tyrone: It hurt. Consequences are high with that lifestyle.

Paula: And today?

Tyrone: It's not trendy to be alone with no nightlife. I am always working on myself now. I am reading and writing for me. I do it to learn as much about why I think like I do and to understand my choices and why I made them. The consequences of doing this work is that I should come out the other side a better person with a super need to motivate myself, and that's a good day for sure.

Paula: What is the benefit of goal-setting for you?

Tyrone: To me, the strength of goal-setting is in setting the right goals and looking at my history to achieve in this area of my life. Then I look at my willingness to work toward the goal. For me it came late, but now I own it and I am a better student of the game. By understanding how and why I make choices, I better understand my skill set in this area.

Paula: What evidence do you have that you are working toward your goals?

Tyrone: Finding my passion is my evidence that I am working toward my goals. At first I knew that I really had a desire to give more of myself to get better. In my career I longed for something to help me find a reason for doing my job besides money. Left alone to do the same thing all day, every day, I was learning but not "getting" it. So *I asked for help*. That was hard to do. It might be hard for anybody, at any level, to admit you suck at something. I did that, then went to my peers and said it. I decided to go after my coworkers' best traits to make them my own. I put an effort in to find what's inside of them. To find out what works for someone else so I could use it. I decided to grind hard to be a better person, and this behavior changed me!

Paula: What is your payoff for working this hard?

Tyrone: There are many. One is finding my passion and what fuels me; it led me to work harder and become a better student at the game of life. I was looking for long-term solutions that I never had done before. I realize I have a chance to make history with me, myself, by finding something in my life I love to do, which is a chance to tell my story. My hope is someone will learn from it and find a passion, then commit to fulfilling it with all their energy. I will work hard to make it happen. Nothing can stop my vision or my dream except me.

Set your long-term goals but don't forget to break them down into smaller pieces.

Setting goals for the future

Many people can describe what they want for their future. The reason many do not attain those dreams is because they fail to set and work toward goals.

What do you want to have accomplished in three months? Six months? One year? Two years? Five years? Ten years?

To accomplish a long-term goal it is important to set short-term goals along the way.

Dissect each increment of time by planning small goals to accomplish in smaller time frames.

Today's date: ________________

Date three months from now.

Long-term goal to have attained by that date:

Short-term goals to accomplish:

Daily:

Weekly:

Monthly:

Date six months from now:

Long-term goal to have attained by that date:

Short-term goals to accomplish:

Daily:

Weekly:

Monthly:

Date one year from now:

Long-term goal to have attained by that date:

Short-term goals to accomplish:

Daily:

Weekly:

Monthly:

Date two years from now:

Long-term goal to have attained by that date:

Short-term goals to accomplish:

Daily:

Weekly:

Monthly:

Date five years from now:

Long-term goal to have attained by that date:

Short-term goals to accomplish:

Daily:

Weekly:

Monthly:

Date 10 years from now:

Long-term goal to have attained by that date:

Short-term goals to accomplish:

Daily:

Weekly:

Monthly:

To have higher quality relationships, don't look for better people.
Become a better person.

Having healthier and more effective relationships

If the same problem continues to present itself in many different arenas, who or what is in need of change?

Communication

What kind of a communicator do you believe you are?

How were you communicated with when you were growing up?

How did you see your family communicate with one another?

Are you similar or different than that? Explain.

Do you believe others hear you when you are sharing? Explain.

Do you believe you hear others when they are sharing? Explain.

Intimacy is often thought of as being sexual. Intimacy is actually an ability to be emotionally vulnerable with another while feeling safe. A good way to think of intimacy is Into-Me-See.

With whom do you feel most comfortable sharing intimately?

What makes you feel comfortable sharing with this person (or these people)?

Talk about people you trust.

Talk about people you admire.

Talk about someone with whom you would like to have better communication.

What currently limits your ability to communicate with that person

We also have conversations with ourselves. That "voice inside of your head" is important in your relationship with others.

What does that voice tell you about yourself?

Positive:

Negative:

What does your voice tell you that you listen to and what makes you listen?

What does that voice tell you that you fail to listen to or ignore? What makes you discount it?

What impact does that voice have on your relationships?

That voice is important to listen to. It can encourage us to be the best we can be or it can convince us we aren't good enough to succeed. What would you like that voice to tell you?

Positive Thoughts	Negative Thoughts

Much of our communication is nonverbal. If someone tells you they are "fine" while their arms are folded and say it in a tone of voice that indicates they are angry, are they saying a great deal without saying anything?

What are some ways you communicate nonverbally when you feel:

Angry?

Happy?

Sad?

Frustrated?

Lonely?

Afraid?

Effective communication

Everyone communicates, but not everyone communicates effectively.

Do you best communicate with people in groups or individually? Explain.

What makes it most difficult to communicate in the other setting?

How might you improve your communication in the other setting?

How important to you is becoming better at communication?

What might change in your life if you communicated more effectively?

Sometimes people fear being vulnerable through communication. What fears might you have about being vulnerable?

____

____

____

____

Don't let people take advantage of you. Set boundaries.
Don't take advantage of others. Respect their boundaries.

Boundaries

Establishing boundaries is important in communication. What are boundaries, in your opinion?

____

____

____

____

Boundaries prevent you from being harmed. An example of a physical boundary might be a fence around your yard to keep your animal inside. Emotional boundaries are similar. They keep you from being emotionally harmed.

What emotional boundaries do you currently have?

Person	Boundary	To protect you from?

Professional boundaries

Circle the areas below that might concern you in your future profession.

Dress	Language	Work ethic	Burnout	Ethics
Client vs. friend	Enmeshment	Understanding	Detaching	

Add your own concerns.

What boundaries do you need to implement and enforce?

Person	Boundary	To protect you from?

What are your concerns about doing this?

Romantic relationships

What is your vision for an ideal mate?

Circle the characteristics above that you possess yourself. If you are not healthy it is unlikely you will have a healthy romantic partnership.

How does your vision for an ideal mate limit your opportunity to find a partner or have a productive relationship with your current partner?

What would your romantic relationship (or future relationship) look like if you allowed yourself to be more open to a "good fit," instead of "your fit"?

We sometimes look into a potential job longer than a potential mate. If you were to write a resume, what would you include?

Previous employment

How long at employer

Reason for leaving

Who should you include? Everyone.

Develop a relationship resume. *Complete the following as many or as few times as needed, beginning with the most recent romantic relationship working backward.*

1. Most recent relationship was/is with: ______________________________

Length of this relationship: ______________________________

Beginning/ending date: ______________________________

Reason this relationship ended:

____

____

____

____

What did you like about this relationship?

____

____

____

____

What did you dislike about this relationship?

____

____

____

____

What would this person say about you today?

____

____

____

____

2. Relationship prior was with: ______________________________

Length of this relationship: ______________________________

Beginning/ending date: ______________________________

Reason this relationship ended:

____

____

What did you like about this relationship?

What did you dislike about this relationship?

What would this person say about you today?

3. Relationship prior was with: ______

Length of this relationship: ______

Beginning/ending date: ______

Reason this relationship ended:

What did you like about this relationship?

What did you dislike about this relationship?

____

____

____

____

What would this person say about you today?

____

____

____

____

4. Relationship prior was with: ______________________________

Length of this relationship: ______________________________

Beginning/ending date: ______________________________

Reason this relationship ended:

____

____

____

____

What did you like about this relationship?

____

____

____

____

What did you dislike about this relationship?

____

____

____

____

What would this person say about you today?

____

____

5. Relationship prior was with: ______

Length of this relationship: ______

Beginning/ending date: ______

Reason this relationship ended:

What did you like about this relationship?

What did you dislike about this relationship?

What would this person say about you today?

When complete, look for patterns of behavior. How long do your relationships last? What is the reason they end? Do your partners have similar characteristics? What did you discover?

A victim blames another person for the place they are in life. If you find your circumstances are the same repeatedly, could it be you?

What could you improve in order to have better romantic relationships?

More introspection

What would you like to learn but up to now have been too embarrassed to try?

How tied are you to your story? Can you possibly change?

Knowing what you know about you, how will you use this information to live consciously daily?

Discuss areas you will commit to improving, eliminating or changing in your life. Note the reason and the plan of action.

Courtesy of Rick Bingham

Courtesy of Rick Bingham

Paula Heller Garland & Tyrone Carrington